Rescue and Shelter Cats

Alex Summers

Rourke
Educational Media

rourkeeducationalmedia.com

Scan for Related Titles
and Teacher Resources

Before Reading:

Building Academic Vocabulary and Background Knowledge

Before reading a book, it is important to tap into what your child or students already know about the topic. This will help them develop their vocabulary, increase their reading comprehension, and make connections across the curriculum.

1. Look at the cover of the book. What will this book be about?
2. What do you already know about the topic?
3. Let's study the Table of Contents. What will you learn about in the book's chapters?
4. What would you like to learn about this topic? Do you think you might learn about it from this book? Why or why not?
5. Use a reading journal to write about your knowledge of this topic. Record what you already know about the topic and what you hope to learn about the topic.
6. Read the book.
7. In your reading journal, record what you learned about the topic and your response to the book.
8. After reading the book complete the activities below.

Content Area Vocabulary
Read the list. What do these words mean?

adopted
commitment
euthanized
goal
interaction
litters
neutering
promote
spaying

After Reading:

Comprehension and Extension Activity

After reading the book, work on the following questions with your child or students in order to check their level of reading comprehension and content mastery.

1. What is the goal of all rescue organizations and animal shelters? (Summarize)
2. What is the difference between a stray cat and a feral cat? (Asking questions)
3. In what ways are cats a great fit for families? (Text to self connection)
4. What are some reasons animal shelters have an application process to adopt a cat? (Summarize)
5. Why does the U.S. have such a high cat population compared to other countries? (Asking questions)

Extension Activity

The United States has one of the highest cat populations in the world. One cause of this population explosion is because owners do not always spay or neuter their cat. Research the cost and importance of spaying or neutering cats. Look up the statistics on the number of kittens born to female cats. Create a visual presentation displaying the importance of spaying or neutering cats to your family or classmates.

Table of Contents

Chapter 1

What is a Cat Rescue?

A cat rescue is a facility that takes in unwanted, **abused**, or neglected cats and dedicates themselves to finding suitable homes for them.

There are probably many cat rescue organizations in your city or town. Cat rescues are no-kill facilities. This means the cats or kittens will be taken care of by fosters until they are **adopted** instead of being **euthanized**, or put to sleep.

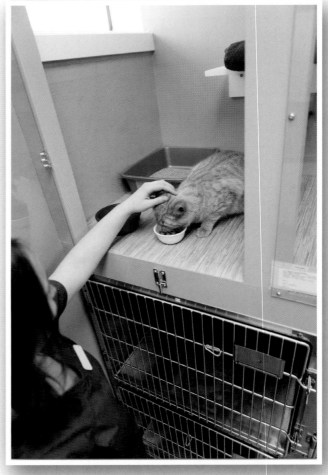

Rescue workers go above and beyond the call of duty to ensure the safety of these unprotected animals.

Some cat rescues focus on special needs cats that are blind, deaf, or have other physical problems that may require just the right person to adopt them.

It takes just the right person to care for a special needs cat but the love they can provide is worth the extra effort.

Some fosters may take care of many cats at one time. This requires a person with a love and dedication for these animals in need.

Rescue organizations have fosters who take care of the needs of the cats while under their care, including litter training, feeding, veterinary visits, and setting up meetings with potential people looking to adopt them.

When cats or kittens are rescued, they are taken to a veterinarian to make sure they are not suffering from any diseases and to see if they have been spayed or neutered. Vets also check the cats for a microchip so if they have an owner they can be notified.

A stray cat is a pet who has been lost or abandoned, is used to contact with people, and is tame enough to be adopted. A feral cat is the offspring of stray or feral cats and is not accustomed to human contact. Feral cats are usually too fearful to be handled or adopted.

FURRY FACT

*The average number of **litters** a fertile cat produces is one to two a year. Each litter averages four to six kittens. It is impossible to determine how many stray and feral cats live in the United States. Estimates range up to 70 million.*

Stray cats can carry many diseases, such as distemper, upper respiratory disease, and rabies. Vaccinating is a way to prevent spreading these diseases to other animals they may come in contact with.

Chapter 2
What is a Cat Shelter?

A cat shelter and a rescue are different in a number of ways. Shelters house stray or unwanted cats in the hope they can find homes for them. However, due to overcrowding some of these animals are euthanized and are never adopted.

Although shelters must cage cats a majority of the time to conserve space, cats are so inquisitive by nature that they enjoy a little playtime or interaction with other cats.

After as little as two weeks in a traditional shelter, cats can begin to deteriorate and become withdrawn, depressed, anxious, or aggressive. If adopted, animals who have been confined for extended periods are often returned because of behavioral issues. This is just one of the many reasons over-population and overcrowding in shelters is such a problem.

FURRY FACT

There are about 13,600 community animal shelters nationwide that are independent. There is no national organization monitoring these shelters. The terms Humane Society and SPCA are generic. Shelters using those names are not part of the American Society for the Prevention of Cruelty to Animals (ASPCA), or the Humane Society of the United States.

Traditional shelters lack the volunteers, funds, and money to give the animals the attention they deserve.

Some shelters are called no-kill shelters, which means they keep the cats or kittens until they can find a forever home. In cases like this, the shelter must rely on donations from their community or money from government agencies to house, feed, and take care of the animals for as long as needed.

Many no-kill shelters hold fundraisers or community events that provide awareness about their organization and help raise money at the same time! Pet stores, such as Petco and PetSmart also partner with shelters by putting adoptable cats in their stores.

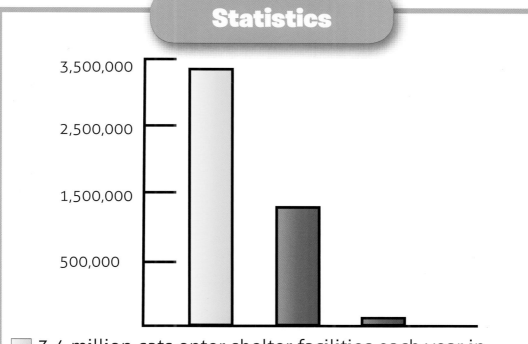

3.4 million cats enter shelter facilities each year in the U.S.

1.4 million cats are euthanized each year in the U.S.

100,000 cats who enter shelters each year are returned to their owners.

Source: ASPCA

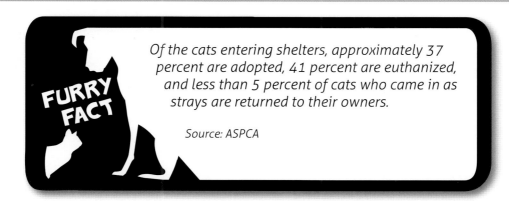

Of the cats entering shelters, approximately 37 percent are adopted, 41 percent are euthanized, and less than 5 percent of cats who came in as strays are returned to their owners.

Source: ASPCA

FURRY FACT

Chapter 3
What is the Solution?

Adopting a cat from a rescue or shelter is a long-term **commitment**. A cute, cuddly kitten will grow up to be a cat and can live for up to twenty years. That's a long time. It takes a lot of responsibility, patience, money, and love to give an animal the care it needs to feel like a part of your family.

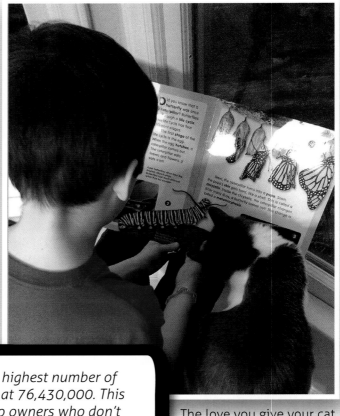

The love you give your cat will be returned with many purrs and snuggles!

FURRY FACT

The U.S. has the highest number of cats estimated at 76,430,000. This is partly due to owners who don't get their cats spayed or neutered causing the population to soar well above other countries.

Rescue and shelter groups can provide advice on making the relationship with your cat the best it can be for the rest of his or her life. This gives you the confidence you need to be a great cat owner!

So now you have made a decision about adopting a cat or kitten. Do some research first to find out what type of cat would be best for you and your family. Make sure no one is allergic to cats and that you will be able to provide a safe, comfortable environment.

FURRY FACT

Twenty-five percent of all animals who are brought to shelters are purebreds. If purchased from a breeder or pet store, purebreds cost a lot of money.

After you have decided on the type of cat or kitten you would like, visit nearby rescues and shelters in your area. Don't get discouraged if you can't find what you are looking for right away. Sadly, rescues and shelters receive new animals every day. If you keep looking, chances are you will find the right match for you and your family.

Spaying or **neutering** your cat helps control the pet population and ensures that the number of unwanted, abandoned, and surrendered cats can be controlled. It can also prevent a litter of unexpected kittens!

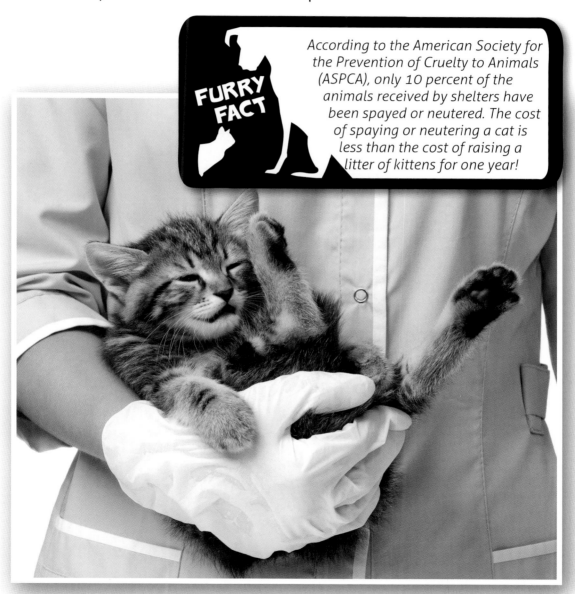

FURRY FACT

According to the American Society for the Prevention of Cruelty to Animals (ASPCA), only 10 percent of the animals received by shelters have been spayed or neutered. The cost of spaying or neutering a cat is less than the cost of raising a litter of kittens for one year!

Spaying or neutering your cat is a common surgery done in a vet's office. It requires minimal after care and you can pick up your cat the same day!

Chapter 4
Before You Adopt!

Adopting a cat or kitten from a rescue or shelter is a big commitment. Make sure you are ready to take on the extra responsibilities owning a cat will bring.

Checklist

Use this checklist to see if adopting a rescue or shelter cat is the right decision for you.

☑ *Do I have the time to play and engage with a cat?*

☑ *Can I afford the medical costs for a cat?*

☑ *Do I have the attention to give to a cat?*

☑ *Do I have the right environment for a cat to live in?*

☑ *Do I have the commitment it takes to make a cat a part of my family?*

☑ *Do I have another animal that may not get along with a cat?*

By adopting a rescue or shelter cat you are saving the life of an innocent animal who will be a loyal, loving companion for many years to come!

FURRY FACT

*Pets can ease loneliness, reduce stress, **promote** social **interaction**, encourage exercise and playfulness, and provide unconditional love and affection. Caring for a pet may even help you live longer.*

Now that you know more about rescue and shelter cats visit a local rescue or shelter and ask for a private visit or meet with a cat or kitten of your choice. When you find that special furry friend, you will know that you are helping save the life of a cat that may have had no other chance.

Bella was adopted March 23, 2005 from the St. Lucie County Humane Society.

Flynn was adopted May 11, 2013 from a local shelter in North Carolina.

Cat and Max's mother was taken in as a stray and were two of four kittens which were kept by the person who took the mother in.

Moxxi was adopted in 2011 in Cañon City, Colorado.

St. Francis Society Animal Rescue Cat Silvie nursing two orphaned kittens.

Willy was only a kitten when he was found abandoned. He was adopted by those who found him.

Owning a rescue or shelter cat will be one of the best decisions your family has ever made!

It is the **goal** of all rescue organizations and animal shelters to adopt out as many of their animals as possible to loving homes. They attempt to keep the cost of adopting down and the fee often includes shots and spaying or neutering. The fee differs with each shelter or rescue. Shelters and rescues are very careful who they let adopt an animal. Some have a long application process, often including references and mandatory home visits.

Do careful research on the type, size, and temperament of the cat you are looking for.

Check your local area for any rescues or shelters before buying from a pet store.

Donate your time or extra money you save to an organization that you feel needs help.

Tell your friends and family about the importance of spaying and neutering their pets.

Do a research paper, opinion paper, or science project giving facts on rescue and shelter cats.

If you find a stray cat, make sure to take it to your nearest shelter or veterinarian to see if it has a microchip that may give information on the owner.

Organize a food drive at your school and collect food and other supplies that you can donate to a local rescue or shelter.

Glossary

adopted (uh-DAHPT-id): to have taken an animal into your family

commitment (kuh-MIT-muhnt): doing a specific thing or supporting a specific cause

euthanized (yoo-thuh-NIZED): ending the life of an animal or person

goal (gohl): something that you aim to do

interaction (in-tur-AKT-shuhn): playing or engaging in something fun

litters (LIT-urz): a number of baby animals that are born at the same time to the same mother

neutering (NOO-tur-een): making an animal unable to produce young by removing its reproductive organs

promote (pruh-MOTE): to make the public aware of something

spaying (SPAY-een): making an animal unable to produce young by removing its reproductive organs

Index

Show What You Know

1. Why is spaying or neutering a cat so important?
2. What are some ways you can find the right cat for you and your family?
3. Which country has the highest population of cats?
4. What percent of purebred animals can be found at shelters?
5. What type of research should you do before adopting a cat?

Websites to Visit

www.humanesociety.org
www.petfinder.com
www.dosomething.org

About the Author

Alex Summers is a true animal lover. Over the years she has had everything from dogs, horses, cats, ducks, rabbits, birds, and even snakes! With two daughters, she feels like animals are not only a learning experience for kids, but a necessary part of growing up. By the way, the snake was not her favorite! She lives in Florida where there are, unfortunately, plenty of slithering snakes!

Meet The Author!
www.meetREMauthors.com

PHOTO CREDITS: Cover: ©dwightsmith; cover (bottom): ©milasupinskaya; cover (top), page 7, page 9, page 13, page 17: ©Kali9; title page: ©Anna Yakimova; page 4: Francois Pilon; page 5: ©absolutimages; page 6: knape; page 8: ©Tom Feist; page 9: ©YinYang; page 10, page 14: ©AKatz; page 12: ©Luana Mitten; page 15: ©Anastasiia Prokofyeva; page 16: ©LindaYolanda; page20: © arhan; page 21 (top): Rob Marmion; page 21 (middle): ©Ljupco Smo; page 21 (middle): TSnowImages; page 21 (bottom): jfmdesign

Edited by: Luana Mitten

Cover and Interior design by: Jen Thomas

Library of Congress PCN Data

Rescue and Shelter Cats/ Alex Summers
(Animal Matters)
ISBN 978-1-63430-065-0 (hard cover)
ISBN 978-1-63430-095-7(soft cover)
ISBN 978-1-63430-121-3 (e-Book)
Library of Congress Control Number: 2014953369

Printed in the United States of America, North Mankato, Minnesota

Also Available as:

ROURKE'S e-Books